Shackled Freedom:
Black Living in the Modern American South

Dasan Ahanu

AQUARIUS PRESS

Willow Books Imprint
Detroit, Michigan

Shackled Freedom: Black Living in the Modern American South

Editor: Randall Horton

Cover Art: Gemynii Evolving www.piecesofagem.com

ISBN 978-1-7357408-1-2

AQUARIUS PRESS LLC
PO Box 23096
Detroit, MI 48223

Willow Books, an imprint of Aquarius Press
www.WillowLit.net

Printed in the United States of America

Dedication

For Mama, Nanny, Grandma, Charles, Joe

For Keenan, Tavis, Will, Tess, Rage

For Black on Black Rhyme, Southern Fried

For Bull City Slam Team, Slam Charlotte

For The Watering Hole

For Us…Down here

Contents

Foreword 7
Preface 11
Introduction 15
The Land They Forgot 17
Black Boy Serenaded in 7 19
Dimepeace 23
Dreams of where the Noose called Home 27

Conversation with God 30
Down Home 33
Bus Ride 35
Painted (Shadow) 37
We (Shadows) 39
For the Quiet Ones 40
5 On the Black Hand Side 44
Change Tin 45
Then (For My Grandma) 49
A Beautifully Imperfect Dedication 53
Black Holiness 54
An Antebellum Love 57
Can We Overcome? 60
Last Time 62
Segregated 1950 64
Learning Black 65
Sun, Moon, and Models 67
Gospel of John 69
Free Association and Funerals 71
Metaphor for Delbert McClintocks 73
For White Poets... 77

Epilogue 78

Foreword

One time, (All stories should begin with "One time…") when I was eight…

Or maybe I was eleven.

I don't know how old I was; it's really not that important to this story except to say that I was somewhere between those tender Black boy years of realizing that I am alive while beginning a life of constantly trying not to die.

Let's just say I was twelve.

Anyway, every spring, my family would spend a week at my aunt Marvell's two-bedroom house that, luckily, was located across the street from the Household of Faith Holiness Church of the Living God, The Pillar and Ground of Truth. (By the way, this story is not about God or church, so relax.)

Because my aunt's house was so small, my mother, two aunts, three sisters, five cousins and I would cram ourselves onto the beds, floors, couches and corners of this tiny brick house across from where we would worship all day and all night for an entire week. My aunt didn't have a television (Everyone knows that televisions are nothing but instruction boxes for heathens) so, instead of watching movies, all of the cousins would stay up all night playing board games and laughing as my oldest cousin Reggie mimicked the Holy Ghost shouts of every saved and sanctified member of the congregation. My aunts spent most of the time cooking.

Around the corner from my aunt's house lived Elder R.O. Johnson, the second-in-command of all seven churches that assembled during this Holy Week. And, because my grandmother was a founding member of the Household of Faith, instead of staying at my aunt's house, she would bunk with Elder Johnson and his wife, a faithful woman who was almost as devout as my grandmother.

The problem with this arrangement was that I loved my grandmother and was not used to being apart from her for any extended period of time. So, occasionally, I would walk the half block to Elder Johnson's house and just sit there quietly, just so I could be close to my grandmother.

Elder Johnson was a stern, intimidating man who seemed seven feet tall and was built like a fire hydrant. (As I grew older, I realized that he was five-foot-six, tops. But you know how it is when you are eight… or eleven… or alive.) He made dry jokes, dreamed of becoming an auctioneer, and owned a furniture store/gas station/extermination business that made most of its money selling candy and cold sodas.

Elder Johnson would let me run the entire store sometimes when I was in town. He taught me how to throw a punch and chop people in the throat. He told me stories about fighting in Vietnam. He gave me a microphone for my eleventh birthday (It really was my eleventh birthday. I remember that part clearly.) One time, I watched him fight a white man who called me a "moon cricket" for counting his change too slowly. He had a dog named "Mutt" who was...You know. Elder Johnson was the closest thing I had to a grandfather (my grandfather died before I was born).

Elder Johnson's wife, sister Johnson, always thought I would be an "important person" one day. So, aside from anointing my head with oil every year to keep me protected, she always urged me to read stuff from her collection of Christian books. Most of it was boring, but there was one series of books that I loved by a Puerto Rican gang member-turned-Christian author named Nicky Cruz.

One morning, during Convention Week, I was waiting to walk with my grandmother to church. Elder Johnson was standing in front of me, tying his tie when my grandmother sauntered out of the spare bedroom. I distinctly remember that there was a James Cleveland record blasting through the house on the hi-fi stereo. Sister Johnson noticed my grandmother and asked her how she slept, to which my grandmother replied:

"I'm pretty sure I fainted in my sleep."

I thought that was the funniest thing ever.

That's all.

* * *

One time, I met Dasan Ahanu.

It was at the Southern Fried Poetry Festival, a four-day event that eventually replaced my childhood church convention as my annual spring trek. That day, his poetry slam team faced mine, in the final bout of the festival. We were in an art gallery and I instantly knew who he was before he even introduced himself. He seemed about seven feet tall because...Well, *he is about seven feet tall.*

That day, I realized why Dasan is known as a "poet's poet." I honestly don't know what that means but everyone says it, so I guess poets own other poets. (I, on the other hand, am known as a "student loan company's poet.") Dasan didn't have a gimmick. He didn't yell, nor did he whisper. He wasn't extremely militant (which I expected because... Come on. His name is "Dasan Ahanu"). Instead, he just writes good poetry.

...*Really good poetry.*

Then we just walked outside and talked about hip hop until the sun went down.

And that is all.

* * *

Most discussions about the combination of activism, social justice and art are usually mired in the bespattered muck of Black pain. Whether it's in grainy cell phone footage, a movie about a slave with a heart of gold, or the pages of a poetry book, it's almost as if Black folks have to bleed out on the immaculately shined floors where white people are free to walk barefoot in order to prove our existence. And poets, more than any other group of artists, are nothing if not willing wrist-slitters sloshing blood everywhere in order to be seen.

The whole of Black existence, however, is not typified by our proximity to death. And for activism or art to ever be successful, it must reflect more of us than our toiling, the tears and arterial gashes. Perhaps there are more ways to celebrate and examine Black life than juxtaposing it with death. We know how to whistle and fry chicken and double-dutch, too.

I know that because, one time, Dasan Ahanu wrote a book of poetry. And it was seven feet tall. And it did not whisper. And it did not scream. It was just poetry…

But really good poetry.

And when I read it, I did not feel like I was bleeding. I was waiting for my grandma on the couch, giggling with switchblade stories in my lap as James Cleveland hollered about Jesus. For that moment, I had forgotten about trying not to die. I was just Black. And alive.

One time, I was shackled *and free.*

And every Black story is a God and a church.

...So relax.

— Michael Harriot

Preface

I started a project called Radical Voice and Artistic Expression (RVAE) in 2014. The goal was to be actively engaged in connecting the art and artists to an integrated strategy for radical transformation.

In *Everything Worth Fighting For: An Exploration of Being Black in America* I defined Radical Voice.

> Radical Voice is defined as a distinctive manner of expression aimed at the root or origin of an issue; favoring drastic political, economic, or social change; and conveying revolutionary and redemptive principles inherent in radical social movements.

This concept of Radical Voice is inspired by a business principle outlined by Albert O. Hirschman in *Exit, Voice, and Loyalty* that identifies "exit" and "voice" as strategies for expressing dissatisfaction with an entity. "Exit" is quitting use or association or switching to a competitor. "Voice" is to agitate and exert influence for change "from within."

When I think of social movements I see them as being vehicles of "voice." They effectively connect their struggle to a source (target) and organize responses toward that source that voice dissatisfaction. These movements also voice solutions and alternatives. I see the art as being so valuable in helping to do this work. Art can help articulate struggle, it can identify and interrogate targets, and it can maintain a vision of change that reminds people of what they are struggling for and what it will look like when they win. So, I push for artists to be at the table helping organizers to see how they can contribute to the planning and execution of strategy.

I want to help artists continue to think about how the work they create can foster transformation. Artists are impacted by the world around them. It influences their work. For artists of color, this is especially true, due to having to negotiate daily the way the world they live in constantly challenges their existence. Their art becomes their outlet. Their expression becomes both catharsis and response. This work is powerful by itself. When coupled with other art across genres, the impact is monumental. That's why when I think about the possibilities, I frame Radical Voice as a multi-genre artistic agitation intended to exert influence and inspire change.

Influencing how people see the world is an important factor in impacting change. Art can affect how people see the world. I know the need for "radical voice" in contemporary art. I believe that part of my responsibility is to create capacity and promote radicalism in art.

RVAE brings artists together to discuss how to integrate their artistic and their creative talents (vision, innovation, analysis, etc.) into movement building and social change. It is also about working with institutions, organizations, and civic partners to facilitate their thinking about how art can help to achieve their goals and better serve the community. Just imagine what can happen when art is an integrated part of work that is focused on bringing about redemptive (individual) and revolutionary (collective) change. There is too much that can be done.

This book is the second installment of a three-part series dedicated to the idea of Radical Voice. I am using my talents to attempt to push back at a variety of rigid narratives about Black life, particularly in the South. My ongoing mission is to widen the scope. I believe that the media narrows our understanding. In doing so, they reduce our existence. That makes it easier for the rhetoric and propaganda used against us to root in our societal consciousness. By expanding the scope, I can present us as layered, nuanced, and dynamic. Through the images and stories shared, I can show how our lives are impacted by the struggles we face in our society.

With my work, I can offer counter narratives to the ways we are too often presented.

—Dasan Ahanu

Acknowledgments

I want to thank Michael Harriott for writing the foreword. It meant a lot to me to have you do that. Thank you also for the convos we have had and the insight shared. You are brilliant, sir.

Thank you to MD Marcus, Wendy Jones, and Redefining Freedom for your eyes on these poems. I trust you to look over my pieces and make sure my editing is sharp. I also value your opinion on the work. You are angels.

Thank you to Randall Horton for years of brotherhood. Thank you for believing in the work. Thank you for all you do.

Thank you to Heather and Aquarius Press/Willow Books for publishing this work. It is an honor to do this with you.

Thank you to Gemynii for the artwork. I want to make sure that as many people as possible know how talented you are. You continue to inspire me. I hope I do the same for you.

Thank you to the organizers who have helped inform my thinking about the impact I can have with my art. You have provided the framework for how I move as an artist and organizer. I am forever grateful for the way you have impacted my life.

Thank you to Angela Lee and Melody Little with the St. Joseph's Historic Foundation/Hayti Heritage Center. You gave me an artistic home. I am so grateful for all the work you have supported and the community you helped me build at that venue. I don't know about anyone else, but the poets are grateful.

Thank you to all the southern artists, scholars, organizers, dreamers, and builders. I am because you are.

Thank you to the South. I wouldn't want to be born, bred, fed, and nurtured anywhere else.

Introduction

I am Southern. I am Black. I am an artist. I walk in a rich, beautiful, and powerful tradition. This book is my contribution to that tradition. It is my way of honoring everyone who helped me understand what it means to be a Black Southern artist. It is a way of repaying the belief in me shown by so many people in my life. The South made me, raised me, and gave me my platform.

From the cookouts to the church house, I have seen the impact of vivid storytelling, passion, and conviction. I have witnessed the power of a good word. I've shared space with some of the most amazing blessings. I have learned from some of the most endearing soothsayers. I carry all of that with me and I funnel it all into my art.

I know some still see Black folks in the South as less than. I see the joy, the struggle, the hurt, the fight, the strength, and the magic. I know that we are so much more than many want to acknowledge. Down here we love, we fight, we dream, and we won't let ourselves be defined in any way that ain't of us, from us.

We are determined down here. We are proud down here. We be full of life down here. As long as I have breath in my body and a pen in my hand I will never let anyone forget that.

—Dasan Ahanu

"I have never liked stale phrases and bodiless courage. I have the nerve to walk my own way, however hard, in my search for reality, rather than climb upon the rattling wagon of wishful illusions."

—Zora Neale Hurston (in a letter to Countee Cullen)

The Land They Forgot

They call joy reckless
where dim asphalt
and heavy shoulders
comprise the
first place
the city
forgot.

A place where
mama's God and uncle
Lester's Jim Beam
make pain easier
to forget.

This place,
where laughter dances
under street lights,
smiles billboard the
corner store, and
hallelujahs fill the
pews beneath stained glass.

A place whose heroes
stand picturesque
on cardboard stapled
to Popsicle sticks or airbrushed
on the front of dulling
tee shirts.

This place, that be
heavily patrolled,
underfunded, and bastardized
because of the black and
brown polymer
used to weave
resilience round these parts.

It cannot be erased;
it cannot be bleached,
burned, or bloodied less than;
it cannot ever be demonized or
stigmatized into disappearing.

We will never let its beauty become
foreign to our eyes, never
let its taste become bland
to our tongues, never
let its smell become any less
than grease and freedom, never
let its sound become any less
a joyful noise, and never
let its touch be anything other
than a welcoming embrace
home.

Black Boy Serenaded in 7

1.
Tomorrow was always further away than
than the trail of one tear down his cheek.
When they told that black boy
to reach for his future.
He just retreated and cried,
water welled up inside.
It was like his dreams were drowning in his eyes.
He's heard them say, "It's ok to let that water flow"
but he knows bout black boys and rivers.
They say remember your roots, they'll help you grow
but he knows bout black boys and trees.
Tell me what is he supposed to do?
When black boy supposed to be
tame, calm, or docile.
Chained, obedient, or on his knees.
'Cause that's how you get a better life black boy.
Don't you want a better life black boy?
Tell him what this better supposed to be.
Life is just a lie that gets effed up worse
if you act in a way that wasn't scripted or rehearsed.
You better bear this burden black boy.
Learn to pull yourself up by your
bootstraps black boy.
Didn't we give you opportunity?
You better learn to exercise your right to be free.

2.
What he's been going through
isn't just fit for anyone.
It's well exercised mayhem.
This sullen soul
doesn't know the price of happy
but he knows they give pain free
to the po', broke, and lonely,
and throw wishes into the water

to learn to swim.
It's different strokes for different folks.
Can't breaststroke with a foot on your chest.
Can't backstroke when they are desperately
trying to erase the existence
of the pool behind you.
Butterflies are beautiful.
The last time he felt that way
was in his mother's arms at the hospital
before social services took him away.
Can't fly with underdeveloped wings.
Can't swim with inoperable limbs.
He runs a butter knife across his wrist.
As committed to suicide as this world
is committed to nurturing his tomorrows.
Don't want you here black boy.
Don't belong here black boy.

3.
You tell a black boy
His survival
only means a rose made it through the concrete.
Making it in this world isn't as hard as it seems.
White lies are truly sincere
Privilege and oppression put him here.
Future taking its last breath in his tears.
See the thing about the other side of town is
momma may have, poppa may have,
but on that side of town
God blesses the child with the residue
of Jim Crow on his skin
never intended to have his own.
The night sky ain't pretty without them stars
black boy.
Them dark clouds ain't a storm
without thunder, white lightning, and rain
black boy.
Dark dirt ain't special.

It's white sands that everyone travels to see
black boy.
Ain't you tired of what you'll never be
black boy?
Blue collar families raising red bloodied teens
chasing a white washed illusion of the
"American Dream."

4.
Black boy begs Death to knock on his door,
come face him on his own terms
because he knows there's too much
of a disadvantage in them streets.
You over qualified black boy.
You under qualified black boy.
We can't approve this application black boy.
You got the job because you fit the description
black boy.
We pulled you over because you fit the description
black boy.
Stop resisting arrest black boy.
Why you running away black boy?
Stay down black boy.
Why won't you wake up black boy?
Black boy sitting in darkness.
Arms holding the last bit of sanity he has left.
No longer wants to face blind judgement
'cause justice can't see how
he's at the ends of his rope.
Societal norms picnicking at the sight
of this strange fruit hanging from
the tree of knowledge
this world don't love him.
Can't talk right, can't act right.
Don't look right, can't be right.
Woke up on the wrong side of the bed.
Grew up on the wrong side of the tracks.

5.
Black boy didn't ask for it, now he asks for it to end.
Picks up a pen, stabs it into his kin.
He wants to write his eulogy.
Wonders if this is how his ancestors
wrote his destiny.
Only the ink never dried, it flows in his veins.
He never writes love stories,
funny anecdotes, only pain.
Wishes the tears would stop falling.
Sad words dancing in the rain
leaving his journal stained.
Believes he is so worthless
Death doesn't even know his name.
He just be another black boy.

6.
I know you worth more, black boy.
I know you mean more, black boy.
So, you survive, black boy.
You shine, black boy.
You write, black boy.
You dream, you hope,
you fight, black boy.
You scream, black boy.
You speak, black boy.
You teach, you learn,
you rage, black boy.
Be spark, be fuel, be flame,
be blaze, black boy.

7.
Black boy in darkness
holding on to the last bit
of sanity he has left.
His only wish is liberation.
I don't want that to die. I mean, I can't let that die.
Don't you see, we can't let that die.

Dimepeace

1.
A tree falls loudly
in a forest with no one around
a deaf man chuckles

2.
Trying hard to forget
he painted his mirror black
it still reflects him

3.
White chalk on concrete
the devil loves to draw
portraits on the sidewalks

4 months after
a black dressed goodbye
A young dreamer with a box
of burst balloons
and a cup of broken pencils
finger paints a Dear John letter
to the blissful ignorance
we tend to hold so dear
Too often she has been betrayed
by lead and pins
so she would rather the message
be delivered by the 5 fingers
of her hand
She wants to feel the words

This brilliant griot is a psychic
and sorcerer
Brings to life the stories
whispered amidst the breath
of the city from 6am to dusk
Some of them come from

an uncle considered crazy
A bellowing empath mocked
for what seems to be
random senility but
only God knows that the exchange
of money and narcotic
is the catalyst for that laugh

This talented wordsmith
Has been writing fantasy
since she was 7
Called a liar by those
who refuse to believe her
when she says her father
was taken by the monsters
in his closet
They just can't seem
to grasp the concept
that the uniforms
hanging there stole his soul
He darkened his reflection
figurin' if he doesn't
have to be reminded of the dreams
in his eyes every morning
he can leave again to do what
he has to do for his family

This lonely daydreamer
has conversations with her
invisible friend often
Those 8 bullets only ended his time
on this earth, not in her heart
She confides in him
every hope, aspiration, and intention
Considers it an honor to live
for her and him
Black boy treated as invisible before
Is just gone now....

She was taught that any man
arm, leg, leg, arm, head
willing to work hard for a week's pay
and get his hands dirty
can poem his life beautiful
Can write his family taken care of
But she has watched each line fall flat
Dead to the world, dead inside, or
dead and gone
9 lines used up, no lives left
None of them destined for published promise
None of them fit for bound spine and happy ending
She paints each haiku in her notebook
like magic
Trying to cast the spell to reverse the curse
her family has become

There is a palette across her fingertips
A mosaic of hope in her heart
A masterpiece on her canvas that says
I am here now
I will be here tomorrow
A will in her spirit that says
Blessings gon' come and
hurt ain't gon' last
A fire in her soul raging with passion
and determination
Heaven's apprentice learnt the marvel
of creation at a young age
So watch her call light out of the dark
Watch her cull life from mud
Watch her raise her passion from the dead
and craft a living everyone will believe in

10.
My God
What a glorious sight it is

to see this artist
at work

Dreams of where the Noose called Home

I look atop a hill and see twins
Arms stretched
Haggard skin
Blowing in the breeze with their friends
They wear frowns now
But I believe at one time they were smiling
Until they had to see those who were brought
Bought
Buried beside their roots
Ain't that what devils do with truth?
A wooden embrace slumped by ropes
wrapped around the throats
of sopranos hung bass notes when caught
Ain't that how you show devils
come covered in midnight
Don't you hang fallen angels as proof?

There ain't been enough kisses in fall
to erase the picnics of summer
Ain't been enough Easter egg hunts
to erase the sound of marched steps
and torches
Daddy tried to tie a swing to a branch once
Twin saw the tire and cringed
Started to bend
First strong breeze
We found that limb on the ground
Tire lying on a bed of leaves
Knotted noose dangling
We didn't know what happened
so Daddy tried it again
It happened again
Why did it keep happening?
Ain't that what we been asking for years?
I guess
That what that tree knew best:

when you're worn down
by all you have had to tread
what you need most is to rest

We played hide and seek there once, twice
But it never quite felt right
We never tried hide and go get it
because the last time someone did it
John escaped
in the middle of the night
with his son and his wife
Them trees
They remember when them men
and hounds set out in the dark
Them trees will always remember
what it means to be found
because they will always carry with them
that bark
They will always remember that crack
When insolence was rewarded
with the portraits
of trees whipped into black backs

Them trees be knowing
See them there trees be griots
Telling tales of the rise that's possible
and the darkness that looms
These trees be tombs
Ask Isis and Osiris bout what
can be raised from them trunks
No, these trees be pyramids
Pointing toward heaven
from roots spread wide
open them up,
ain't the riches of rings
and the wisdom of ages found inside?

They tell me that some used to say

everything you needed to know about faith
was in them woods
Cuz when you in them fields
don't you dream them trees split like Red Sea?
Ain't that big house where Pharaoh be?
Ain't the other side of that forest
like New Testament?
Don't them leaves fall and resurrect
three months later?
Didn't they have church in the clearing?
Wasn't them stumps the first alters?
Pastors elevated to spread that gospel
Ain't they been replacing God with men?
That there be an evangelical forest

Momma Nature say look at her babies
See how they've grown
She say they father been known
for Immaculate Conception
but rarely do he get credit for tending
to these others
Them twins ain't fooled
Devils want them believed bastards
So that when they get chopped down
don't nobody cry for sap spilled,
for their sisters and brothers killed
Ain't that real familiar?
Me and them trees be kindred
Me and them trees be understanding
That's why when we meet
both haggard, heavy, and frowning
We be happy to see each other
still standing

Conversation with God

I heard a poet ask God,
"What's it like to get all of the credit
but none of the blame?"
Immediately I wondered if he recognized
the oppression in his inquiry
If he noticed the white washed
atheism on his tongue
as he so casually took the Lord's
place in our consciousness in vain
Because ain't no way anybody
with skin of bronze and hair of wool
would ever get to take glory without the shame
That there be a trick question

My God made peace out of chaos
Made life out of mud
Made family out of imagination
Had his truth co-opted by snakes
Seen his hard work turned tragedy
Forced to clean up the mess
Rebuild from nothing but what
he could stash for a rainy day
Had a baby out of wedlock
Watched his child be raised by another man
Saw him persecuted for his abilities
Martyred by a system afraid of him
My God has watched this world
bend his name to its will
and call it conviction
Seen men put him to work as gospel
for a privatized prosperity
We are not speaking to the same person

They hung my God from trees
They immortalized yours in stained glass
and hung him in living rooms

to remind us we will never be fit
for gated community
until we repented from our sins
Sin we are born in
Ain't that like black skin?
Your God took his son and
made him shepherd over a flock
of folks with faces like midnight
and hair of wool
Ain't that like nepotism?
My God watched his son
be elevated as good shepherd
for laying down his life
for those he was giving care of
Ain't that like charismatic leadership?
How come they never die of natural causes?
Ain't target they calling and tragic they last name?
Tell me poet
Who is it you are speaking to again?

This is the problem with white liberalism
A leveling of the playing field
becomes parking lot
when paved with the asphalt of black skin
But that lot ain't fit for others
until they draw white lines?
Ain't that what it means to be civilized?
Ain't they been teaching us compartmentalization?
From the top of a building
don't the empty parking lot look
like the hull of a slave ship?
I bet executives get to work early
to watch laborers park on black backs.
I wonder if it feel like overseer?
Do they ever hear the pavement gasp?

Sorry poet
Ain't no "amen" for you here

Your words feel too much like conquest
Like sitting amidst my tribe
with a forked tongue truth
I wonder if your pen feels like rifle
Would you give it to me to use
if I brought you my people
as barter?
And no, it would not be better
if you darken the language
I have seen what happens
when white folks stuff
black people in passages
Putting them on stage as barter
for anyone paying enough attention
Ain't our lives just another cash crop?

This is the problem with post racial rhetoric
It becomes the perfect hiding spot
for selective memory
The perfect platform to attack
an illusion rather than
call oppression by name
When has white patriarchy ever
believed in accountability?
When has privilege ever
turned down acclaim?
Doesn't white supremacy still
see us as everything wrong here?
Even as we have overcome
the subjugation, bigotry, violence, and pain?
When you ask who is God
to get all the credit and none
of the blame
Remember that the God
you are speaking to
and the God that speaks through me
are not the same

Down Home

They act like the sun shine different down home
Like the dirt too dark for repentance
Like civilized stop at the Mason Dixon
They say guilt dense as fog, east of the Mississippi
Say it sho' sound like selective amnesia round here
Say you can still smell the ash in the air
Plantations, crosses, hay, trash
Pit cookers, stump hole stills, churches
But don't we walk like resilience in spite of?
Smile like a belief in the up on high?
Laugh like cotton was tickling
the field hollers out of us?
Each house is a hymnal down here
Each penny colored cheek is a joyful noise
You know, the kind a noose is supposed to silence

Down here is a boot camp for the forgotten
Mud trudged, weeds pulled, dirt dominated
We know planting, tilling,
picking, feeding, feasting
We know ain't no tomorrow
better realized than by hard work
and redemption
We know that backwoods
ain't the opposite of progress
That dirt roads don't mean deserted
That hospitality ain't a subtle surrender

Down home,
we know they see us as natural disaster
I say ain't we calm in the eye of a hurricane?
Ain't we the American Dream's
guilty conscience?
Ain't we the best example
of make something out of nothing
To wade in the water and swing low?

Ain't we a blues lick
and a second line reverie?
Ain't we joyful noise on Sundays?
Ain't we chitlin' circuited genius
from Gulf to the Great Lakes?
Ain't we spread on the table?
Ain't we the clothes on your back?
Ain't we the yesterday you want to
so desperately forget
and the tomorrow you can't make
without us?
Ain't we magic?
Ain't we here?
Ain't we gon be here?
Ain't we?
Ain't we life, love, joy, overcoming,
glory, glory Hallelujah?
Ain't we an amen?
Ain't we?
Ain't we?
Amen

Bus Ride

We sit side by side.
Passaged in the middle of this bus.
Quiet.
She wears black.
I am.
We, are
strangers.

The early morning sun is
trying to mediate us comfortable.
No words are exchanged.
Yogurt mixed and scooped
into mouth.
Bagel unwrapped and pulled
in half.
Two brown bags crumbled
in unexpected syncopation.
Shoulders slumped
in considerate accommodation.
We both know shrinking
for others.
Both know
a backup singer's harmony.
We eat in silence.
Sit
silent.

Two by two along the left
like comrades with a
marching determination.
Two by two
like Noah's taming obedience.
We are a blinded balance
who have unfairly judged this
moment too awkward to trust.

Technology transports us
to post racial distraction.
Bitten apples identify the
escapes in our hands and laps.
The devil is in the detailed
dedication to screens.
Like we will know all things.
Like we aren't ignorant to how
we have been conditioned
to hide.
We type
silent.

Time passes. Our gated
communities uninterrupted
until a clumsy spill of tea on her
white Converse becomes
a mocking irony.
One her washing machine
will try to make invisible.
Like it never happened.
Like new. Like make great
again. Ironic isn't it?
How privilege teaches its own to do the same.
A ritualistic separation heightened
with bleached ignorance and
cold hearts.

The bus stops.
We arrive at our destination
and exit
silent.

Painted (Shadow)

There is a shadow
who wishes to be a painting
Spends most days
a Black box too used
to being adaptable
Who sees trust as
suspension of disbelief
and puts on a
revolving schedule of shows
to rave reviews

I call this shadow my name
Cover its shoulders in colors
Sometimes detachable
Set aside when rooms don't feel
art gallery enough
Put back on for the admiration
of visionaries
who know how to make
Black canvas holy
Who see adornment as
joyful noise

There is a shadow
who wishes to be a painting
Spends too many days
a darkroom used for
realizing everyone else's
visions
One who understands the
value of solution
Knows how to develop,
stop, and fix
One who carefully
washes cheeks clean
and can hang 1000 words

in the air to dry by the light
whether sun or fluorescent
or spot

I call this shadow my name
Cover its shoulders in colors
buttoned up and draped free flowing
Replaced when rooms don't feel
art gallery enough
Coordinated perfectly for the
admiration of visionaries
who know how to make
Black canvas holy
Who see portraiture
as testimony
Who see opening receptions
as exercises in
self-determination

I be a nuanced shadow
too large to be missed
too dulled at the corners
to be menacing
All those years of smart,
mannerable, and good
All those bedtime prayers
momma sent skyward to God
that her baby would be safe
A shadow who puts a reverie
over shoulders
burdened by the call
of misguided dreams
And carries that chorus
to wherever there are
believers needing to be
reminded what worship
sounds like

We (Shadows)

We be shadows
Like a night ripe for imagination
Our smiles
are glorious train cars
waiting to carry the good news
Our bodies are towering walls
anxious to be more than
ash dulled facade
Graffiti written in beautiful hues
Can't you see the names
of every insecurity and
every affirmation
covering head to toe?

We face tribulations
like a midnight hail storm
Like a wrong time, wrong place black body
gasping a final will they remember my name
Like black and brown trauma
Like the night sky was trying to remind folks
that pummeled don't always
leave bruises, but it still hurts

We be ticking time bombs
Here to remind them
that a gated community
is no different a predatory industry
than a prison yard.
That a clock face
Is just eyes wide shut
and justified paranoia.
That the hands that dictate the hour
are on borrowed time
once those on the outside
realize that what's on the inside
is surrounded by numbers.

For the Quiet Ones

I have placed my voice in the hands of those
who have crafted their own script for it
Lent it to those who have admired it from afar
and daydreamed it at their disposal
Sacrificed it as offering to the gods of make peace
cuz ain't nobody listening no way

I have watched this voice be confused so much
it doesn't know where home is
Can't remember its way around anymore
Gets lost trying to find the path out my mouth
I have found it screaming to get through my smile
or felt it banging on my chest
Crying in the palm of my hands,
or trying to escape through hard work
I have looked into the eyes of the quiet ones
and know we both see a familiar reflection

I have thought about evicting this voice
On days I have been my weakest
I have blasphemed it broken
Said they could have it,
but NO
It is mine

It will not be silenced by ventriloquism
It will not be cast in an adaptation of me
It will no longer use silence as barter
to end conflict
It will not accept repetition
as the only means of understanding
It will not accept repetition
as the only means of understanding
It will not accept repetition
as the only means of understanding
You will not make it scream

to be acknowledged
Promise it freedom
and then demonize its liberation
The weary it wears in its tone
is not a mark of your success

Listen
No, no listen again
What you hear is rebellion
What you hear is the toppling of a rule
that put us in margins,
took our tongues as barter for broken promises,
and called us complicit
What you hear is a rallying cry
that called a funeral procession of words forth
out our lungs
until the parade of purpose
became a new speech, a new dialect,
a new articulation
of the worth we've always held,
but will never let you discount again

On behalf of all the hushed miracles
digging through the landfills
of other people's crap
to find the self-determined melody
we were made to throw away
I want you to know that this,
this is an eventual goodbye
and a we won't be thinking bout you
when we gone
It is a well-placed ignorance to
the pronunciation of your name
whenever anyone considers a conversation
an opportunity to seance your ghost
It is a Dear John letter never signed or sent
Matter of fact, we smashed the mailbox with a bat
Burned it and the stand it stood on

until the cinders and darkening metal
became the end of a witch hunt
for your approval

Then,
we and our voices danced
around that fire in hushed ceremony
until the flames tempered
the frigid you made our voice boxes

Oh yeah, we talking now
We singing now
Only this is for us and not you
Because I've come to understand
you don't deserve not na'an syllable
Ain't fit to know the love notes
above the clef of our chins
Ain't fit to know the dreams
behind our eyes
Ain't fit to know the fight
in our hearts
Because if you never bothered
to listen in the first place
What is there to miss
when it's all gone?

They say the greatest trick
the devil ever pulled
was convincing our words
that they don't exist
I say the greatest retaliation
is to make sure those same words
go missing
when that narcissistic angel
has fallen and cries
to the heaven of our insight for
redemption and answers
My God,

what a power we now know
belongs to us
Tell me,
ain't it deafening?

5 On the Black Hand Side

1.
Daddy, when will they
value Black life? When
it's sold on EBay

2.
Oppression's greatest fear?
A Black Queer woman
with a plan and a bullhorn

3.
When Reagan dropped "Welfare Queen"
It also went pop
and took over the airwaves

4.
I don't know the riches
of the tombs of Pharaohs
but I know that big glass bottle
of change sitting in
the corner of mama's bedroom

5.
Big mama ain't never
known no other love
than full and whole and God

Change Tin

My Nanny kept quarters in an old coffee tin
Treasure chest filled with blessings
and labeled in hallelujah
It sat on a shelf in the cupboard
by the basin my Nanny used to wash
Black women's burdens away
A hairdresser on evenings and weekends
Diva on most days
Usher on Sundays
She was the hardbound cover of a book
I liked to pretend God read by moonlight
each evening

Me
I was a vagabond of curiosity
A mischievous young prodigy
who loved to ramble
loved to discover,
open and peek inside
Spoiled by the 'you give and I take'
of adorable adolescence

I remember when I first learned the meaning
of blasphemy
That was the day I stole an arcade's worth
of treasure from the tin
To me it was a great adventure
A pirated betrayal I could never imagine
the impact of

When I got back from spending
everything that wasn't mine
I was faced with a look
that for so long after
I tried to pray out of my memory
What was haunting about it

was not that she told me
I could've just asked for it
It was that she was baffled at how
I thought she wasn't going to find out
when I had no way of putting it back

Since then I've never held on to anything
I couldn't replace before anyone knew it was gone
or held on to anyone long
without putting them back

I learned a lesson about reciprocity
I don't take anyone's kindness,
belief, or support for granted
Won't turn my back on responsibility
Ain't gon' slack when I show up
Gon' make damn sure I provide
opportunities for those who are
coming behind me

I've seen what happens when people take
and don't give back
When a treasure chest
is left empty with no care or concern
A pirated betrayal that others never
bother to consider the implications of
For every bit of shine I get
I give back every piece of insight
I have to offer

That's why I am so adamant about
nurturing talents and gifts
I don't just see potential
I see a change tin
filled with blessings
and labeled in hallelujah
I know the value of what's inside
Know that anyone willing to

let me show them how
to fill their coffers
will learn how to earn dollars
and give back change

See I learned a lesson about selfishness
I don't take anyone's time for granted
Won't take advantage of anyone's desire
Won't take what anyone sees in me lightly
Gon' make sure to think deeply
before committing to taking anyone's heart

I know the haunting look of a face
that is left wondering why
I took what I wasn't able to give back
with absolutely no regard
for the outcome
Only caught up in the satisfaction
of the moment

That is why I've been single
for a long time now
Because when I look
into her eyes
I see a change tin
Filled with blessings
and labeled in hallelujah
I refuse to take what is inside
without first asking her and God if I should
If the answer isn't as resounding
as my Nanny's Sunday cooking
then the only option
is a respectful goodbye

That's just the dollars and sense
of the situation

Some folks say I talk in riddles
Some say I think too much,
that I'm too analytical
I'm just a vagabond of curiosity
who loves to ramble
Loves to discover,
open and peek inside
but best believe that I'm
extremely careful with what I find
Extra cautious with what I reach for
Will not leave with what I can't bring back
Because by the coffee table in the living room
of my memory
is an easy chair where God sits
just over my right shoulder
I know that he is
waiting for the right time
to remind me of that wayward child
and the southern sage
he called home
The one who taught
me the meaning of reciprocity
with a change tin

Then (For My Grandma)

There will never be another dawn
Only your smile
There will never be another storm
Only your tongue
No seasons changing
Only your relentless dedication
to the babies you opened
your home to
There will be no night
No dusk
Just the comfort of your living room
The sustenance of your cooking
There will be no time passed
No calendars
No clock ticks
Just the fight in your spirit
to the very moment
you finally allowed
yourself to rest

There will be nothing
No more
No later
No next time
There will be no now
Only then
For the rest of our time here
each then will remind us
of the powerhouse you are
Whenever we feel you too far away
Each then will take us back
to the last happy
No now
Not today
Only then
That is the only certainty I can lay claim to

This here today is just
a lesson to pay attention to the "thens"
we might have taken for granted
The last subtle nudge on your way
to a better stomping ground

Now I apologize if this seems awkward
Not quite sentimental enough
There are not enough pretty words
Not enough metaphors or similes
Not enough heaven
for your insight
Not enough life after for the hearts
you have touched
You tell them to remodel
Not enough room for the souls you
showed the meaning of grace
Tell them from here on out
they gone have to
add an extra greeter
at the pearly gates
Not enough laughs
Never enough time

I won't let go of then
Any then
I'll pick the one I need most
to fight back the
end I'll want soon
if it means another then
with you
No now
Not today
I'll never let go of then
Never past
Never yesterday
Yesterday is blasphemy
Just then

Just right
Just you
Forever more

I don't know how I'll do tomorrow
No more tomorrows
Just another gift from God
I'll know why they keep coming
He ain't ever had a voice
in his right ear like yours
We been knowing
Now HE knows too

See this ain't bout what's no mo'
This bout what will never leave
Because you left us with all the thens"
we will ever need
Planted all the seeds
to forest a fantastic future
for the favored who felt your touch
Today ain't no obstacle
The day after ain't neither
Because those "thens" are ever ready
We can share them and reminisce
We can hold them and rejoice
We can reach for them to refill
You were a glorious too much
We are a grateful thank you

I ain't got to get too deep
because we ain't never had
to say too much
to know what was needed
Never no wasted words
Never no wasted moments
Won't be none now
Just "thens" and going on

Soon this will be done
But we will still be here
That means you are still here
They can get lost in this
I am going to stay there
then
Remembering everything you
poured into this rambunctious
and precocious child
And I'm gon show the world
who you were and
who you shaped me to be
You raised mountain movers
Raised earth shakers
Raised builders and nurturers
Carried God's grace and God's wrath
A marvelous warrior
who showed me how to show up and show out
I ain't even begun to spread the good news
Because if they don't know it now
They will know it then

A Beautifully Imperfect Dedication

For my whole career
I have been trying to write
the perfect poem for my mother
Only to realize that she is
the perfect poem

That's it
That's the highlight of what
I've come up with
Simple lines I'm sure
other poets have danced with
Have sat and looked after
with the same smile
our savior spreads across the heavens
when he looked at the earth below
and on the seventh day
said, "It might be GOOD"

But she is GOOD
This poem isn't about my mother
It's about how she deserves
so much more than this poem
Because to me
she is
perfect

Black Holiness

Ain't no glory like lifted voices
Crescendo like burning sage
rifts
Like whips and auction blocks
runs
Like late nights through Bayous
moans
Like lost days in classrooms,
last days on street corners,
Sundays spent praying for
the blessed assurance
you gon' see another sunrise
Ain't that sound deep and guttural?
Ain't it song?

If there is one truth I know
Ain't no heaven like a Black woman's dinner table
Ain't no hallelujah better than redemption songs
All charcoal and shotgun
Ain't no almanac for the notes you learn painful
No census for the massive of that reverie
No recipe for the way melody, molasses, and butter
make Jesus' harmony leavened
Don't it feed you like loaves and fish?
Don't it sit in your chest like hung on cross?
Won't it come back when boulder burdened by silence
Ain't it prettier than Easter service?
We call holy random, spontaneous,
but ain't it just right time, right place?

Ain't that love as proud and specific
as who made the stuffing and potato salad?
Don't it smell like pearly gates opened?
Feel like liberation rang the doorbell
They say you can find our Lord and Savior
on the right hand of God

Then you can find that matriarchal choir
on the left
Gossip and memory never sounded so glorious
Laughter made you believe tomorrow was possible
Smiles made you think hate
was a boogeyman for another night
Ain't no glue like a Black woman's belief
She say it's gone be ok
It be
She say it's in God's hands
It be
She say food is served
It be

It be an alter and an anarchy
Ain't no glory but God's
Ain't no rule but theirs
It be a sanctuary and a sermon
A boot camp and a blessing
Where you don't question the authority
You know when to fall in line
You take orders as they come
This battalion be they babies
no matter the age
This meal is a strategy
we are thankful for
So very thankful
Ain't no better lesson in leadership
than plate made
Ain't no better gratitude
than plate clean
Ain't no better reminder
than seconds served
Here we learn that there is
always more work to do

Didn't Moses and Aaron spend
40 years in the wilderness

before making it to the Promised Land?
Ain't it a Black woman's magic
that reduced it to only 6 days?
What a miracle it is
The way they gather us like disciples
Scripture us family
Teach us that faith can move us forward
whether blood or promised before pastor
whether adopted or seeking admission
Family without works is a flatlined blasphemy
That ain't what they made us for
Ain't no excuse a good enough amnesia
Ain't no trouble a strong enough divide
That table be affirmation that the best
of what we are is a full meal

When that song stops
Ain't ailment nothing but Judas?
Ain't crucifixion just a teary eye home going?
Ain't the three days after
your last hope?
Don't them tears fall in rhythm to that song?
Don't you sing along without ever noticing
how easily the notes come?
Ain't that the best gift you have ever been given?
To know what that hymn sounds like,
what it feels like?
To know what that kitchen supposed to be like?
If there is one truth we know
Ain't no heaven like a Black woman's dinner table
Ain't no hallelujah better than redemption songs
All charcoal and shotgun
All magic and miracle
All Black
and Black woman
Beautiful
Blessed
Beloved

An Antebellum Love

They say beauty is in the eye
of the beholder
In mine you should see
a reflection of all the good things
God perfected when he crafted you
Painted you along a horizon and
told Mother Nature to teach
me the beauty of dawn
A panoramic view
I am thankful to bear witness to
A patchwork mosaic of
YOU
Of us
Of everything right and righteous;
blessed and blasphemous;
satiating and sanctified

I been waiting on you
Praying to the night's sky
that the day would come
when you arrived to
tell me deliverance was on the way
Sat fireside by tree stump
listening to the pastoral
preoccupation my heart
has with you beloved
Don't they say that religion
was given to learn us
satisfied with less than?

But in the dark I found
the glimmer of hope I see
mirrored in your eyes
I can't help but believe
in a resurrected optimism
Ain't that the reward for the convicted?

To be removed from affliction
and given grace from Heaven?
Ain't I been convicted of bad choices?
Been afflicted familiar with goodbyes
But ain't you blessed from on high?
I don't know no other welcome
than to sing your praises

My swung low chariot
who taught me to steal away,
go down Moses, and
wade in the water
You helped me find escape
on the other side
of a shackled belief
I ain't supposed to be
no more than slave
Taught me that emancipation
ain't on the tongue or fingertips
of those who want me
to credit them for
recognizing me worthy
It's in the survival
of my hope and my optimism
until I find the relationship
that sees me equal
Not 3/5 of the illusion
they won't let go of
You and me,
we make love like abolitionists
You hold me until I
forget about sharecropping
Letting go of the liars
who try to still lay claim
to the land you now work
I am grateful
I have met a woman
who kisses like Tubman

Holds me resolved like Sojourner
Moans me faithful
like Pentecost
I consider the distance
between us an
Underground Railroad
My blessed opportunity
to set my heart free

Can We Overcome?

I am at this bar across from a daydream
with eyes like a Birmingham jail
Held me captive long enough
for me to envision an opus
that would move us closer
to overcoming this barrier
to a monumental love
Forced to face the realization
that she sees me lesser, unworthy
Me sitting in with the hope
that she will understand the
humanity of the man I am
She say it's gone too far
I ain't worth equal footing beside her
at an altar down an aisle
All I'm good for is midnights and hard labor,
then back to the other side of town
I want to fight what I feel
but non-violent resistance
is the only way I can imagine
a change that's best for the both of us
I want church in the holy of her heart
She wants me to march the Selma
and Montgomery along her thighs
until our moans become chants of jubilation

I can't stop hoping, dreaming
knowing optimism can quickly become desert deceit
That illusions can take hold
when you've become parched
since the last wet taste
Thinking that maybe you might would
rather be dehydrated
Hell, I just wanna indulge
with the one I promise the rest of my life
I mean if there is a dawn

then there damn sure
is gonna be another night
But I'm thinking too deep
We was here having a civil conversation, right?
Here I am tripping like
I don't know how to act

Last Time

There is a special kind
of absurdity in
the way she thinks.
All Louisiana basin.
With the right
amount of seasoning,
passion, and temperament
to never let the muck
of the world harass the holy
she possesses.
That something special
that weakens your knees
and beckons your hallelujahs
as the call and response
to her shoulder leant to
touch yours.

There is a certain sense of
reckless abandon in the way
she parses rose beds to say things
that make dawn the only
adequate response your smile
can muster to fit this moment.
Where the only thing
you can hold onto is the hope she
appreciates it enough to
bud bloom pucker you happy
so perfunctory.

There is a wisp of a wish
dangling from the back
of a dandelion that you
both watch disappear along
the horizon with hands clasped
and hearts beating.
An anxious melody that

your frontline eyes try to
improv calm over.
Only to be betrayed
by a wind that knows
you are both overcome
by the realization that today
is today and tomorrow
is a goodbye you will never
recover from.

Segregated 1950

My purpose
My love life
Segregated
Like white only
and black only water fountains
I battle with the privilege of one
while fighting for the freedom
and happiness of the other

Learning Black

Never stop dreaming. Nightmare is just another word for expectation. You are worthy. You are valuable. Be valuable. Read. Listen. Grow. Become more valuable. Know your worth. Adjust. Fit in. Be chameleon. Be malleable. Be bright. Be smart. Smile. Excel. Beam. Bright. Be unintimidating. Be articulate. Be well mannered. Say yes sir. Say yes ma'am. There is pride in them dimples. There is legacy in that walk. Walk like you know you somebody. Stand like you know you somebody. Stand tall. Stand straight. Stand up for yourself. Know when you don't belong. Be mindful around white folks. Know when you outta place. Be respectful of elders. Know when you outta line. Be quiet around police. Know when you almost outta time. Don't waste time. Don't stop dreaming. Nightmare is just another word for perception. Work. Work. Work. Only way to have is to earn it. Only way to earn it is to work. Ain't nothing wrong with a hard day's work. Ain't no shame in a job. You got a job to do. Do your job. Do theirs too. Do something. Do it all. Do more. Remember self-care. Know your potential. Don't waste your gifts. Don't take your blessings for granted. Use them. Give back. Give. Remember self-care. Love. Be love. Be mindful everyone ain't love. Say goodbye when necessary. Say hello when possible. Be open minded. Be open door. Don't be door mat. Remember self-care. Let it go. Let her go. Let it be. Trust. Question. Don't be paranoid. Don't be skeptical. Trust. Trust God. Let God. Pray. Faith without works is dead. Live. Dream. Don't stop dreaming. Nightmare is just another word for rejection. You are worthy. You are valuable. Push. Learn. Grow. Become more valuable. Be priceless. Want something. Be dedicated. Be free. Learn that commitment is both. Be committed. Know you are worth it. Know it when it comes. Be willing when it arrives. Believe. Believe in you. Maintain. There is a day waiting for you tomorrow. Be ready. Survive. Get there. There will be another one waiting the day after that. Promise to see that one too. Dream what it will be like. Make it real. Nightmare is just another word for concession. Trust your mother. Trust your father is there. Don't be naive. He is there. Know him when you be him. Be aware who it really is. Know you have seen the results. Change the outcome.

Be sorcerer. Be magic. Don't be magical. It's a trap. Don't be spell cast. It will wear off. Don't be rose colored lenses. Don't be escape hatch. Know your worth. Don't overcharge. Don't undersell. Never auction without appraisal first. Someone's expectation is not your reality. Someone else's tongue is not your own. Accept no other version of you than your own. Accept no other rewards than your own. Know that what is for you will be. Never stop knowing. Never stop dreaming. Nightmare is just another word for death. Don't die until you do. Live like you know you will. Live.

Sun, Moon, and Models

They say that in the midst of a blackout
a neighborhood gathered
in a playground with lit promises,
raised their voices in jubilation,
and lifted candles to the sky.
There, a dim night learnt
the meaning of a great light and
came to understand a joyful noise.

They say that over the shoulder
of a dismissive authoritarian
there was a rising frustration
building in students who were destined
to beam brilliance.
There, bright promises determine that
their success would be a rebellion.
Their graduation will be an event horizon.

Between a community's genesis
and a tomorrow's dawn
I have come to see the blessing
of a promising day
and the power of a revolutionary night.
I know what God's craftsmanship looks like.
Know where to find radiant eyes
and resilient smiles
that remind me of the sun and the moon.

Each week here is a fashion show.
Between every morning
and another midnight
is a curtain waiting to open
to remind us of our magic.
Calling us to catwalk to an affirming applause.
Will crafted by experience and vision.
Survival sewn.

Tradition and history patchworked.
All into a glorious couture.

How can you not believe
you are of a beautiful kind
when you have models all around.
Leaders who show us
that fashion forward
is a stylish strength.
Dreamers who show you
that an eclipse just gives the sun
time to remember its purpose.
Warriors who remind you
that dusk is not an ending.
It is just the bottom of a page
that when turned will reveal
that words are waiting
at the top of the morning.
Silence is never an option.

There are days that can't be called
anything other than inspirational.
There is no mannequined complacency here,
no prepackaged apathy.
Here, a resilient courage exists.
A determined flare for the transformational.

Dressed in be bold,
outfitted in been amazing,
and accessorized
in ain't gone be made to be any less.
My God,
isn't it fabulous?

Gospel of John

One southern midnight,
I noticed a crow
on the shoulder of a monument
honoring a confederate general
in the middle of a park
grown rich green and
fertilized by Black blood.

Watched it shit on the shoulder
of a drunk white man
in layers of frayed cotton
propping himself up
against the statue.

He is so drunk with guilt
he does not notice the shit
over his shoulder.

Southern hospitality and
Grandmama's kitchen table sermons
lead me to ask if he is ok.

He says he is better than me.

I laugh at the irony.

I tell him he needs to eat something
to soak up the white tears
too strong a proof
for him to keep himself composed.

I offer him my pancakes
covered in mammy's syrup
and a blessing.

He told me to go to hell.

I am not surprised
at how he felt my loaves and fish
were a blasphemy.

How false idols, ritual, and spirited escape
had robbed him of his ability
to recognize truly
the face of God.

I left him there begging
a false prophet for an exorcism.

Knowing he will remember
our exchange as healthy dialogue.

Knowing he will consider
the passing of time as progress.

Knowing he will wake in the morning
and call his hangover
post racial

Free Association and Funerals

Hashtag
Target

Hashtag
A word or phrase preceded by a hash or pound sign (#) and used to identify messages on a specific topic.

Target
A mark or point at which someone fires or aims.

Description
A spoken or written representation or account of a person, object, or event.

Fit
Fix or put (something) into place.

Manipulate
Control or influence (a person or situation) cleverly, unfairly, or unscrupulously.

Fit the description

Black Man
Black Woman

Fit the description

Hashtag
Target

Noun
Verb

Black Man
Black Woman

Adjective
Noun
Compound noun

Fear
Hate

Action
Reaction

Hashtag
Target

Reaction
Action

Target

Say name
Proper noun
Bury
Verb
Proper burial

Hashtag

Type name
Proper noun
Symbol
Descriptive noun
Representative burial

Either way
Collective noun
Dead
Gone

Metaphor for Delbert McClintocks

I'm in the bathroom one morning
getting ready and as I run the water and reach
for my toothbrush
I notice something dangling, suspended
just to my left
It's about three inches above the toilet
in the corner of the bathroom
My eyes focus and immediately I tense
It's a damn spider

My heart beat quickens
I am starting to get a little frantic
I immediately scan the room to see how
best to swiftly eradicate this threat
I settle on a paper towelettes
It's easy, encompassing, clean
Grab, squeeze, and then casually
throw in the trash with no remorse
Perfect

I do consider letting it be for a moment
Wonder if we could possibly cohabitate
in this house without violence or disruption
I think briefly of a family
Little cretins waiting for Daddy to come home
Funny how it's always a daddy
Like momma couldn't have spun as functional a web
Like momma couldn't have made the trek here
with as much determination and diligence
My fleeting patriarchal sense of compassion
was shorter than an animal planet commercial break
It had to die

I'm afraid of spiders
I have been since I was a child
I see them in the house

They gotta go
I see them in the car
Either they go or I gotta go
Get missing before I find them
The car gotta go
There are no other options
I see a spider on the outside of my windshield
I contemplate if I ever have to get out
I worry of sneak attack

This fear means that the spider
can never survive
It doesn't matter that I'm bigger
I've watched National Geographic
It doesn't matter that I have the control
I've heard about spider bites
Seen webs everywhere
Hate running into them
Why they gotta be there…outside
It's gotta be me or them
I've seen Spiderman
Seen what contact with them
can change you into

It's funny tho
I only kill them when they are
in places that belong to me
Only in spaces I claim
Spaces I hold authority over
If I see them it's a confrontation
I must win
It doesn't matter what kind of spider it is
I don't see value in knowing its background
I already know that there are dangerous spiders
and any one of them I see fits the description

I mean, I don't normally look to kill things
Well, just bugs…

Bugs in places I didn't invite them to
Bugs that don't look like me
or look like those I like or respect or love
They are othered things
And I hate spiders the most
Some say they are necessary
Some say they have value
Say that there are things that bother me
They are willing to deal with, work with, handle
I don't care
They should know to stay away
or they will die

Now,
I've never been bitten by a spider
Never been attacked
though I call it that when I run into its web
Disrupt its neighborhood
Destroy what it built
Interrupt its work, its life
I've never seen a spider in a menacing pose
Never seen it reach for a weapon
Just look scary, just look like danger
I've never given warning
But it knew I was there
Never saw it raise its legs
Must've be preparing to retaliate
Never given it rights
Only considered my survival right and just
Time is of the essence
I call it a life or death situation
Doesn't die on the first squeeze
It's resisting
Didn't close the paper quick enough
It's running, trying to escape
Fleeing is a violation
I smash it against the wall
Lethal force is now necessary

I've made a mess
But, there are more than enough ways
to clean it up after
Either I or someone else will do it
Make it go away
I just gotta explain my side
Nobody cares about any other
Judge me for what I've done
and I'll be acquitted
After all, it's just a spider
Aren't there more than enough of them
Hell, are there really any good spiders
anyway?

I will tell everyone it was a struggle
That danger was imminent
That the stakes were high
That I had to act quickly
That it should have complied
and stayed away or complied and died quickly
I will say it was a threat
Was probably up to no good
Hanging there about to cause problems
or get into trouble
They will listen to my report
Call it following protocol

Somewhere someone will sing
an itsy-bitsy memorial
Someone will wonder if spider is coming home
A bunch of eyes will find out how vicious fear is
How being somewhere
where someone else thinks you don't belong
can leave empty web
as remembrance
like chalk outline
on asphalt

For White Poets when Rainbows, Colored, or Girl is not Enuf

Some will not listen.

1. So we will write loud and resilient. We will speak Birmingham, Bayard, Lorde, Rivera, Brujas, Sleeping Car Porter, South Bronx, Wilmington, MOVE, our truth, our truth, our truth.

2. We will recognize that colonialism can be grant funded, can charge at the door, can win board seats, can look good on video, can rename hallowed ground conference or workshop or slam. We will understand that some have taken imperialism and renamed it programming.

3. We will understand why shade has never set right with the Black of us. Because shade trees are where they gawked at gasping angels and called it right and just. Our trauma and pain has been fit for applause for years.

4. We will understand why collateral damage has never set right with the rest of us. Because we have been treated as an unintended consequence of this art form. Seen their allyship become urban renewal. They easily propagandize the benefit in the rising property value of their representative voice and page. It is a gentrification we have seen before.

5. We will gather like church basement, like wood clearing, like fireside, like ring shout, like corner cypher, like dinner table, like juke joint. There we will teach craft. We will train alchemists. We will love. We will heal. We will grow.

6. We will realize that some have made this art adornment and claimed it validated them royalty. We will burn their thrones. We will melt their crowns and use them to craft carafes for their tears. For too long reverence has been their hiding place. For too long they've worn us like armor and held us close like shields.

Some will not listen. We will never quiet. They will hear. They will know. They will learn.

Epilogue

"It's like this though…I'm tired of them closed minded folks…It's like we gotta Demo tape but don't nobody want to Hear it, but it's like this…The South got something to say! That's all I got to say."

—Andre 3000 at the 1995 Source Awards

We still talking.

About the Poet

Dasan Ahanu is an award-winning poet and performance artist, public speaker, community organizer, educator, scholar and emcee born and raised in Raleigh, North Carolina. He is an Alumni Nasir Jones Fellow at Harvard's Hip Hop Archive and Research Institute, resident artist at the St. Joseph's Historic Foundation/Hayti Heritage Center, and visiting lecturer at the University of North Carolina-Chapel Hill. He has performed across the country, appeared on national radio and TV, published three books of poetry, been featured in various periodicals and released numerous recordings. He works with organizations and institutions to develop effective arts strategies to enhance their work in the community. Dasan is currently managing a grant funded initiative as the Rothwell Mellon Program Director for Creative Futures with Carolina Performing Arts. He swings a mean pen and represents the SOUTH.

CPSIA information can be obtained
at www.ICGtesting.com
Printed in the USA
JSHW020329190621
16053JS00001B/4

9 781735 740812